Exploring Anglo-Saxon times

World history

Ancient Egyptians (3000–332 BC)

Ancient G

This may have been what England looked like in early Anglo-Saxon times. Much of the land was still forest. The Anglo-Saxons first settled by rivers, because they came to England by boat.

Anglo-Saxon timeline

Anglo-Saxons
raid England

Anglo-Saxons settle
in England

King Raedwald is buried
in his ship at Sutton Hoo

| 350 | 450 | 550 | 650 |

St Augustine is sent to England by the Pope
to convert the Anglo-Saxons to Christianity

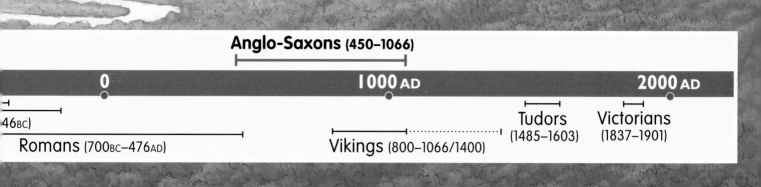

Anglo-Saxons (450–1066)

0   1000 AD   2000 AD

46BC)

Romans (700BC–476AD)   Vikings (800–1066/1400)

Tudors
(1485–1603)

Victorians
(1837–1901)

Contents

Look up the **bold** words in the glossary
on page 32 of this book.

Offa builds Offa's Dyke
to separate England
from Wales

The Great Viking (Danish) Army
arrives, led by King Guthrum

Harold II is king of England.
6 January–14 October 1066
– The Battle of Hastings

750   850   950   1066

Vikings raid England

Vikings and Anglo-Saxon King
Alfred divide England in two

William of Normandy
takes over England

Meet the Anglo-Saxons

This picture shows you what it might have been like to see the Anglo-Saxons rush at you through the forest.

The Anglo-Saxons **conquered** the lands we now call England. They took it from the Romans and the British who lived there before them. The Anglo-Saxons were people from north-western Europe who began to **invade** England while the Romans were still in control, over 1,500 years ago. So they knew they had to fight to gain land and they were fearsome warriors.

The Anglo-Saxons were people who came over to England in small groups, or clans. They never came as a massive army. Each clan had to claim the piece of land it wanted.

Although we use the term Anglo-Saxons, the people who came over from Holland, Germany and Denmark were Angles, Saxons and Jutes.

They ruled England for about 500 years (100 years longer than the Romans). The Angles gave their name to England.

These are the routes the Anglo-Saxons used to reach England. The main tribes were Angles and Saxons, with some Jutes.

North Sea

East Anglia

Mercia

Wessex

Angles
Saxons
Jutes

Where did the Anglo-Saxons come from?

Rich and poor

The Anglo-Saxons lived in warlike times. The stronger and more ruthless you were, the better off and more powerful you became. It was a world in which a few people became very rich, but most people were pitifully poor.

Early Anglo-Saxon clans were ruled by chiefs. As a chief won more land he became more powerful. The most powerful chief became king of a large region. Below the king were the lords. They owned large areas of land, that would later become shires (counties).

Most other Anglo-Saxons were freemen. They farmed their

Nobles and warriors were wealthy as they were the ones who collected the booty from raids. For battle some wore an iron helmet and chain mail, but most wore thick leather coats and helmets.

lord's land and kept most of the food for themselves, but also had to work for their lord. They could also be called up to join the part-time Anglo-Saxon army.

The Anglo-Saxons had slaves to do the hardest work. The slaves were people who were defeated and captured in battle.

- Men needed a 2m long spear, a round shield of wood covered with leather. You would only own a sword if you were a warrior.
- Most people wore simple clothes made from linen and wool. They were coloured using plant dyes. Everyone wore leather shoes and woollen stockings.
- Wealthy people kept warm using a cloak, fastened with an expensive brooch.
- Everyone wore good luck charms.

This is how the ordinary freeman farmer (called a karl) and his family dressed.

Q What did they use to colour their clothes?

The ship burial at Sutton Hoo

Before they became Christians, the Anglo-Saxons believed that when you died you went to the hall of the gods.

If you were a king, it was important to take goods with you so you could hold up your head with pride before the gods. The most important thing that a king owned was a ship – so when a king died, a large pit was dug, the ship dragged into it and the king's body was placed in the ship surrounded by his goods. The whole ship was then covered with soil to make a high burial mound.

One of the most important ship burials was found at Sutton Hoo in Suffolk.

Did you know…?

- That the Sutton Hoo ship is huge – some 30 m from bow to stern and nearly 5 m at its widest.

The final moments of the ship burial of a king. The whole ship, the king and his grave goods are being buried under a mound of soil.

Q **Why was a ship used for burial?**

What was in the grave?

The treasure found with the ship burial at Sutton Hoo tells us much about the way that royal Anglo-Saxons lived. For example, there was a sword with gold and jewel fittings, a heavy gold buckle, large silver dishes made in the Middle East about 500 AD, and a set of 10 silver bowls from the Mediterranean. So this tells us that the Anglo-Saxons traded widely across Europe.

The small pieces on this frame (not the frame itself) is what was left of the king's helmet in the grave...

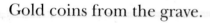
Gold coins from the grave.

Did you know… ?

- The treasure included ornamental purses and gold coins, a battle shield, gold weapons and armour, ornaments, silver, tableware and drinking horns and, rarest of all, a battle helmet.
- Mounds like those of Sutton Hoo were widely known to be the resting places of chiefs and kings and that they contained treasures. This tempted people to rob the graves of their treasures. As a result, most burial sites are empty.

... and this is what the helmet probably looked like when new.

Q **Why were gold coins found in the grave?**

Did you know... ?

- The forest was important to the Saxons. It gave them wood for houses, fuel for their fires and was a place where wild animals could be hunted.
- The only stone building in the village may have been the watchtower so people could keep a look out for attackers.

Untouched forest land.

Saxons were worried about attacks from raiders and wild animals. They protected their villages by building an earth wall around them and topping it with pointed stakes.

Land cleared for farming, farmed in strips.

Defensive bank and ditch

Church

Water mill

Reeds for thatching

Anglo-Saxon villages

Can you imagine what it would have been like to live in an Anglo-Saxon village in the 8th or 9th century?

The village would have been just a few different families. At that time there were no local supermarkets, so these people had to find everything they needed for themselves. They had to have water, food, fuel for heating and cooking, and something to make their homes and clothes.

Water could come from a river or spring. If they were close to a river they could use boats to get about. However, they had to choose places that did not get flooded!

All their food came from what they could grow in the fields next to the village.

Water meadows for livestock grazing.

River

Boats drawn up on shallow bank

Q **What did the villagers use the forest for?**

13

How can you tell where Anglo-Saxons lived?

Many of the places the Anglo-Saxons took over or founded are still used today.

The first Anglo-Saxon villages were commonly named after the chieftain who first won the land. These places end in 'ing' or 'folk', such as Hastings (the place of Haesta's people) and Suffolk (the people of the south).

Most later villages were named after the nature of their surroundings rather than the name of the chieftain. You can spot these in names ending 'ford', 'ham', 'ley', 'ton' and many others. So Oxford means a place where oxen were driven across a ford in a river.

A few places were named after **pagan** gods, such as Wednesbury (which means 'Woden's hill').

Westley

Barking

Westport

Earlston

Stanham

Q Do you have any villages or towns near you that contain Saxon words?

This map contains some typical Anglo-Saxon town names.

Barrowcombe

Penstowe

Longbury

Torsted

Southwich

Anglo-Saxon place names		
Anglo-Saxon	Meaning	Examples
barrow	grove, wood	Barrow-in-Furness
bur, bury	fortified place	Banbury
burgh, burg	castle	Bamburgh
bourn, burn	stream, spring	Bournemouth
dean, den	swine pasture	Ipsden
dun, down	hill, downland	Dunston
grave, grove	grove	Wargrave
ham	homestead	Wolsingham
hurst, hirst	wooded hill	Chislehurst
leigh, lee, ley	glade, clearing	Burnley
mer, mere	lake, pool	Ellesmere
port	market town	Bridport
stan	stone	Stanford
stead, sted	place, site	Stansted
stoke, stock	place	Stokenchurch
stow, stowe	meeting place	Stowmarket
ton, tun	enclosure, village	Tonbridge
wick, wich	dwelling, farm	Norwich

Anglo-Saxon homes

We have to guess what Anglo-Saxon homes were like because they have almost all rotted away or been burned down.

Anglo-Saxons mainly lived in small single-roomed huts. Nobles and even the king simply lived in larger wooden huts. (We call the larger buildings 'hall houses'.)

The houses were built with timbers gathered from the nearby forest. The walls were made of oak planks, or a mesh of twigs (called **wattle**), made windproof with a coating of mud, straw and dung (called **daub**). Some were made with stone. It all depended on what was close at hand.

Milking cows

Spinning wool

People lived in simple houses and did some of their cooking inside. But it was dark inside the house and they spent much of their time outside. This is a harvest-time scene.

Did you know… ?

- Some Anglo-Saxon homes had a sunken floor filled with straw for winter warmth, and as somewhere to store things (a kind of cellar).
- Most roofs were made from thatch. In places where reeds could not be found for the thatch, turf was used over strips of wood bark. In some cases small slats of wood, called shingles, were also used. There was no chimney, just a hole in the roof.
- Any window openings would have been covered with thin animal skins or thin parchment. These let a small amount of light in and helped to keep out the cold of winter.

Threshing corn

Tending pigs

Cutting logs

Q **How many rooms did an Anglo-Saxon house have?**

Anglo-Saxons ate, lived and slept in one room together with their animals.

Did you know... ?

- Peasants caught eel, perch and pike from rivers. Those villagers close to the sea could catch sea fish, such as herring. They were not allowed to hunt the wild forest animals, because they were owned by nobles.
- To preserve meat and fish through the year, it was dried, salted or pickled. Cheese was made from milk – a good way of preserving milk over the winter.
- Barley was used to make weak beer, which was drunk instead of water. The rich had wine shipped in from the Mediterranean.
- Animal fat was valuable for making oil for lamps and **tallow** candles.

Food and drink

If you were an Anglo-Saxon, you ate what you grew. Anglo-Saxons grew carrots, parsnips, cabbages, peas, beans and onions. The rich could pay for spices, such as pepper, imported from distant lands. Fruits included apples, cherries and plums. Honey was used to sweeten food.

Wheat was difficult to grow so most people grew rye which they made into a dark, heavy bread. Only the rich ate wheat bread like us.

Sheep and cows were only killed for meat when they became old because they were needed for milk and wool.

Why would you keep animals in your house?

The Anglo-Saxons become Christians

Where do we come from? What made the Earth, the sky, the food we eat? These are the sorts of questions the Anglo-Saxons asked themselves, just as we would today.

They came up with an answer: they were controlled by superhuman people – gods and goddesses. They also believed that they were directly descended from their gods, such as Woden, Thunor (Thor) and Freyr. Some of our days are also named after early Anglo-Saxon gods – Tiw (Tuesday), Woden (Wednesday), Thunor (Thursday) and Frigg (Friday).

In 597 AD monks were sent by the Pope to convert the pagan Anglo-Saxons of Britain to Christianity. They reached the Scottish border in 635 AD. Over time the Anglo-Saxons became Christians. On the borders of Scotland and England, at Ruthwell, you can see an early cross which still has Anglo-Saxon writing (**runes**) on it.

This is the Anglo-Saxon preaching cross preserved at Ruthwell.

Did you know… ?

- The Ruthwell Cross between Carlisle and Dumfries was carved by skilled Northumbrian sculptors in the early 8th century. It is the most important Anglo-Saxon cross in Scotland.
- It is a teaching cross designed to help people remember key ideas about Christianity.
- Two sides are carved with scenes from the Gospels. The writing is in Latin and could only be read by the monks.
- The sides are carved with vine leaves and animals. The runes (which could be read by the Angles) say 'Dream of the Rood (Cross)'. This is an Anglo-Saxon poem about the crucifixion. This poem talked about Christ as though he were a warrior being put to death.
- Old Scots was inherited from the language the Angles spoke in this borderland.

Q Can you name one Anglo-Saxon god whose name is used for a day of the week?

Church, monks and records

Anglo-Saxons rarely built in stone because the Anglo-Saxon period was mainly one of great violence and struggle.

Their only stone buildings were churches and watchtowers. Watchtowers were minicastles, built to see raiders coming at a distance.

The Anglo-Saxons could retreat in there and defend themselves.

Some still survive, because they were strong enough for churches to be built on to them.

The church, or abbey, was the place where the monks lived.

Monks could read and write and some of them began to write down, or chronicle, their life and times. These **chronicles** tell us much about Anglo-Saxon life and times.

Who wrote about life and times in Anglo-Saxon days?

Tower entrance

Did you know... ?

- Many towers had upper rooms that could only be reached by a ladder. Stones could be thrown down and arrows fired from the top of the tower.
- The most famous monk of these times was the Venerable Bede. He wrote a history of Britain.
- The main records of the time are called the *Anglo-Saxon Chronicles* (diary), the *Lindisfarne Gospels* and *Bede's History of the English People*.

The door to the tower at Earls Barton in Northampton is high up on the wall. It needed a ladder to reach it.

The Vikings attack

In the ninth century the shores of England were attacked by Vikings.

For half a century, the Vikings made hit-and-run raids on the coasts. They came ashore in their **longships** and raided villages, taking their food, the treasures from their churches, and capturing some people and taking them back to be slaves.

The Vikings from Denmark then decided to take over the Anglo-Saxon lands and settle in England. In 865 King Guthrum of Denmark brought over a huge army and landed near London. Then Guthrum's army spread out, taking over Anglo-Saxon lands in eastern England.

A raid by the Vikings on the Northumberland coast.

At first, no Anglo-Saxon king was powerful enough to stop the Vikings. But eventually King Alfred of Wessex was able to gather an army to stop Guthrum. However, both Anglo-Saxons and Vikings were evenly matched and Alfred could not defeat Guthrum. So they agreed that Guthrum would keep the east and north of England, while Alfred kept the south and west.

Did you know… ?

- The Viking raiders were dreaded because they were such good fighters and also because it was impossible for the Anglo-Saxons to know where the Vikings were going to attack next.
- The area where the Danish Vikings settled was under Danish laws. It was called the **Danelaw**.
- When a truce was declared, Alfred started to put walls around his towns, so they would never be overrun again.

Q Which Vikings attacked England, the Norwegian or the Danish?

Anglo-Saxon 'new' towns

What would you do if you were threatened by invaders who had captured half of your country? This is what the Anglo-Saxon King Alfred had to ask himself. The Vikings controlled all of the east of England, an area that became called the Danelaw.

Alfred decided that the best thing to do was to provide some safe places that his people could retreat to and defend if they were attacked. Each had earth walls and wooden stakes on top. They were built at places which were easy for people to get to. So in times of peace they were also good places for merchants to live and trade their goods. As a result, they quickly became rich towns.

The towns were still small. But at the time they were new towns, the streets often laid out to a plan.

Did you know… ?

- Many places fortified from Anglo-Saxon times have names that end in 'bury'.
- Fortified coastal ports end in 'wich', as, for example, Norwich and Aldwych, the Anglo-Saxon part of London.
- A typical town might be about 40 hectares and laid out with a **grid-iron** of roads. Merchants built their houses along these roads. At least one church was also built.
- Towns might need nearly 2,500 men to defend them – far more than lived inside its walls. This is why all landowners in a region had to provide men for an army if asked.

A fortified Saxon town built on the orders of Alfred the Great.

- Lindisfarne
- NORTHUMBRIA
- DANELAW
- Offa's Dyke
- MERCIA
- WESSEX
- New towns

Q **Why did Alfred have walls built around the new towns?**

The end of Anglo-Saxon times

In 1066 the newly crowned Anglo-Saxon king of England was King Harold II. But two other leaders also wanted the crown. It would be a battle of strength to see who would be king.

On 8 September the Viking king, Harald, sailed from Norway and attacked York, in the north of England. King Harold rushed there with his army and on 25 September he defeated the Vikings, killing most of them.

It was bad luck for Harold that, at almost the same time, Duke William's army sailed from Normandy. So Harold now had to rush back south.

The two armies, Anglo-Saxon and Norman, met near Hastings. The battle at first was a stalemate. Then William told his archers to fire into the air, over the Anglo-Saxon shields.

Harold was killed and, without a leader, the Saxons were defeated and William won the battle of Hastings. The land was taken away from the Anglo-Saxons and given to Norman nobles. The time of the Anglo-Saxons was over. It was 14 October, 1066.

Early stages of the battle with cavalry and foot soldiers.

Did you know… ?

- Just before the battle near York, Harold said: "I will give Harald just six feet of English soil; or, since they say he is a tall man, I will give him seven feet!" (meaning just enough room for a grave).
- Harold's army was tired from its battle with the Vikings and they also had to march an enormous distance to get to the south. William's men, on the other hand, were fresh and ready for battle.
- Legend tells of an arrow striking Harold in the eye and killing him. It is more likely, however, that he was simply killed in the battle.

hARO L D REX IN T

The end of the battle. Harold is killed. This picture may show him with an arrow in his eye.

Q **Who won the Battle of Hastings?**

Try these...

Anglo-Saxon costumes

Make a costume from the items shown in these pictures:

Anglo-Saxon boy

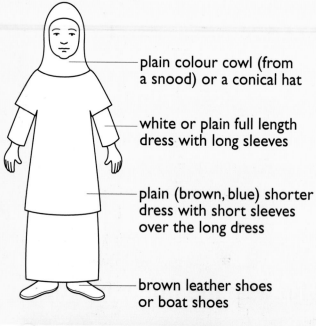

- woollen hat with top tipped towards front
- brooch
- long sleeved shirt – plain colour (green, brown, red)
- brown leather belt
- cape (blue or brown) made from blanket or curtain
- plain coloured trousers (brown, green, red)
- cloth wrapped round legs
- brown leather shoes or boat shoes

Anglo-Saxon girl

- plain colour cowl (from a snood) or a conical hat
- white or plain full length dress with long sleeves
- plain (brown, blue) shorter dress with short sleeves over the long dress
- brown leather shoes or boat shoes

Anglo-Saxon brooch

The Anglo-Saxons had a range of different brooch designs. We know about them because of the metal remains of the brooches. They did not rot away like the clothes they held together.

- Make a copy of one of the brooch shapes below.
- Glue the shape to a piece of card, and cut it out carefully.
- Make a design on the front. You can use plastic beads for jewels.
- On the other side of the card attach a large safety pin with sticky paper.

Anglo-Saxon words

Here are some Old English words for parts of the body. This was the language of the Anglo-Saxons. The words next to the English words are spelled to help you say them as they may have sounded. They may not be spelled like the words used in Anglo-Saxon writing.

Try and learn the words, then play a 'Simon Says'-type game to test how well you know them.

English	Anglo-Saxon
arm	airm
back	back
cheek	hairgospind
chin	kin
ear	eare
elbow	elnboga
eye	eyege
face	neb
finger	finger
forearm	elm
forehead	hnifel
foot	fort
hair	har
head	hafela
leg	barn
nose	nosu

Make a ship burial

- Take a kitchen roll tube and cut it in half lengthways. Use one piece for the main body of the ship (**1**).

- Cut the other piece in half crosswise. Cut out a triangle of cardboard from each piece (**2**). These two pieces will form the ends of the ship.

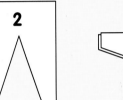

- Fold the cut end of one of the ship ends together (**3**). Then tape the folded ends together with sticky paper.
- Stick each end in place with sticky paper (**4**).

- Make small Plasticine models of grave goods and place them in the centre of the ship.
- Take a box or large dish and place the ship in the bottom. Cover it with sand.
- Now carefully remove the sand to get a sense of what it was like for the archaeologists to uncover a ship burial.

Glossary

chronicle A diary of events. Saxons chronicles were written by monks and so were, in part, to do with religion as well as historical events.

conquer To take over a land by force using an army.

Danelaw The land controlled by the Danes after the Viking invasions. The Saxons and Vikings were closely related and many of their laws were similar, so living in the Danelaw was really little different to living in the rest of England.

daub To cover or smear something with a soft substance, for example a mix of mud, dung, straw and hair.

grid-iron A pattern of roads that cross at right angles.

invade To arrive with an army against the will of the people already living in the land.

longship A ship which used both oars and a sail. It was the biggest, and longest, of the ships that the Anglo-Saxons and Vikings built. It was meant as a kind of battleship.

pagan A word used by Christians to refer to those people who had many gods and spirits.

rune The word comes from an early Anglo-Saxon word *runa* meaning 'secret'. It was an alphabet made from lines joined together at sharp angles.

tallow A hard fat made from parts of the bodies of cattle, sheep, or horses. It was used to make candles and soap.

wattle Willow twigs woven to make a sheet and then used in walls.

Index

Curriculum Visions

Curriculum Visions is a registered trademark of Atlantic Europe Publishing Company Ltd.

Atlantic Europe Publishing

Curriculum Visions Explorers
This series provides straightforward introductions to key worlds and ideas.

You might also be interested in
Our slightly more detailed book, 'Anglo-Saxon raiders and settlers'. There is a Teacher's Guide to match 'Anglo-Saxon raiders and settlers'. Additional notes in PDF format are also available from the publisher to support 'Exploring Anglo-Saxon times'. All of these products are suitable for KS2.

Dedicated Web Site
Watch movies, see many more pictures and read much more in detail about the Anglo-Saxons at:

www.curriculumvisions.com
(Professional Zone: subscription required)

First published in 2007 by Atlantic Europe Publishing Company Ltd
Copyright © 2007 Earthscape

Author
Brian Knapp, BSc, PhD

Educational Consultant
JM Smith (former Deputy Head of Wellfield School, Burnley, Lancashire)

Senior Designer
Adele Humphries, BA

Editor
Gillian Gatehouse

Photographs
The Earthscape Picture Library, except *The British Museum* pages 10–11, *The Granger Collection, New York* pages 28–29.

Illustrations
Mark Stacey except p5 and 27 (maps)
David Woodroffe

Designed and produced by
Earthscape

Printed in China by
WKT Company Ltd

Exploring Anglo-Saxon times – Curriculum Visions
A CIP record for this book is available from the British Library
ISBN 978 1 86214 209 1

This product is manufactured from sustainable managed forests. For every tree cut down at least one more is planted.